POWERING THE HOME

Fifty years of advertising
home appliances (1920–1970)

Ruth Artmonsky & Stella Harpley

Published by Artmonsky Arts
Flat 1, 27 Henrietta Street
London WC2E 8NA
Telephone: 020 7240 8774
Email: artmonskyruth@gmail.com

ISBN 978-0-9935878-1-8

All Rights Reserved
Copyright 2016 Ruth Artmonsky & Stella Harpley

The cover design for this book is respectfully adapted from the cover illustration for *'Joy! A gas fire in the bedroom!'* which is found on page 68 of this book.

Opposite: Enamel badge, Mr. Therm designed by Eric Fraser c1931
Opposite contents: Poster detail c1930s

Designed by Webb & Webb Design Limited
Printed in England by Northend Creative Print Solutions

CONTENTS

- 9   Introduction
- 11   The Gas and Electricity Industries
- 29   Cooking
- 43   Cleaning
- 55   Lighting
- 65   Heating
- 75   Entertainment
- 91   Epilogue
- 94   Bibliography

INTRODUCTION

hen researching a book on the advertising and selling of furniture, I found the subject matter expanding dangerously, to such an extent that the intended small book was likely to morph into an encyclopaedia. I decided to discipline my curiosity by setting up a firm boundary, and it was by this that I found it necessary to exclude domestic appliances from my definition of furniture.

Meanwhile, as every compulsive ephemera collector will understand, the accumulating of ephemera on powered domestic appliances went on unabated as I couldn't resist such morsels as an advertisement for a gas iron, and a rare one of a man admitting he might be able to do the laundry when the house purchased a washing machine.

Having completed the furniture book, these surplus ephemera would catch my eye from time to time until the temptation became too much; I decided to give them their own book. Here it is!

Gas Exhibit at Austin Hall, Wembley, 1924

THE GAS AND ELECTRICITY INDUSTRIES

Individuals were experimenting with gas and electricity, and the appliances that could be powered by them, long before anything resembling an 'industry' came into being. If one looks at gas alone, a Scot, William Murdoch, was recorded as installing gas lighting in his home as early as towards the end of the 18th century, but it was not until the middle of the 19th century that gas producing companies or authorities could be said to be nation wide, and even then mainly focused on selling gas for street lighting, factories and public buildings. By the time gas was nationalised, with the Gas Act of 1948, there were literally over one thousand undertakings manufacturing gas or gas appliances, from one man bands to what was claimed to be the biggest such organisation in the world – the Gas Light and Coke Company.

When it came to the domestic use of gas, initially gas producers had considered it enough merely to pipe gas to houses and leave it to the householder to find the appliances needed.

....
Cosigas advertisement, *Ideal Home (detail)*, 1962

But finding very different standards in the actual production and installation of appliances, often with negative commercial repercussions, the industry began to supply appliances as well. From the late 19th century the gas industry showed its wares and usages at exhibitions and began to employ women, mainly with some sort of home economics background, along with male chefs, to demonstrate at exhibitions and in local showrooms that were starting to open across the country which offered both the hire and sale of appliances.

It wasn't until the arrival of electricity as a competitor, [or rather the notional threat of electricity as a competitor, for electricity was slow to domesticate itself], that the gas 'industry' began to appreciate the need for a more active approach to the advertising and promotion of its products. The British Commercial Gas Association [BCGA] was formed in 1911 – a cooperative body which aimed to represent all branches of the industry, funded by the industry, and run by a representative body drawn from the industry. It presented itself initially in an advisory capacity –

Poster by Septimus E. Scott for the British Commercial Gas Association, 1925

'...at the service of the public for advice and help on any subject large or small, connected with the economical use of gas in the home, office or factory.'

But obviously BCGA's aim was rather more than advisory; it was to sell – to present gas and gas appliances in the best possible light and to persuade the public to buy. BCGA was lucky enough to have a number of highly competent and evangelic people at its helm from the start, who were able to act effectively in a rather conservative industry not always ready to take up the ideas and methods of a rapidly developing advertising industry. Francis Goodenough of the Gas Light and Coke Company, who was to act as Chairman of the BCGA for over 20 years, was an early management and marketing devotee rather than a technical gas man, went by the adage 'it is no use manufacturing cheaply what you cannot sell'. He brought, to a sceptical industry, the urgency to use advertising in addition to exhibition and showroom publicity. Press advertisements began to appear in both national newspapers and general interest magazines – the BCGA is said, at one time, to be placing regularly in some 30 journals and some half dozen newspapers.

Mrs. Maud Adeline Cloudesley Brereton was another personality key to the early activities of the BCGA. Having worked at a women's training college and with an interest in public health and sanitation, she was appointed BCGA's staff writer and editor of its monthly magazines – *The Bulletin* and

British Commercial Gas Association advertisement, *Punch*, 1923

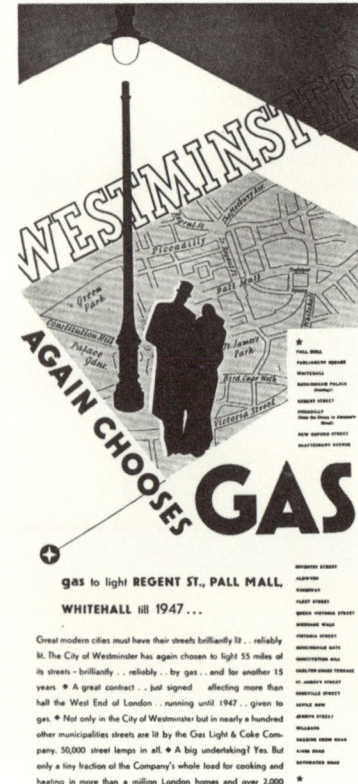

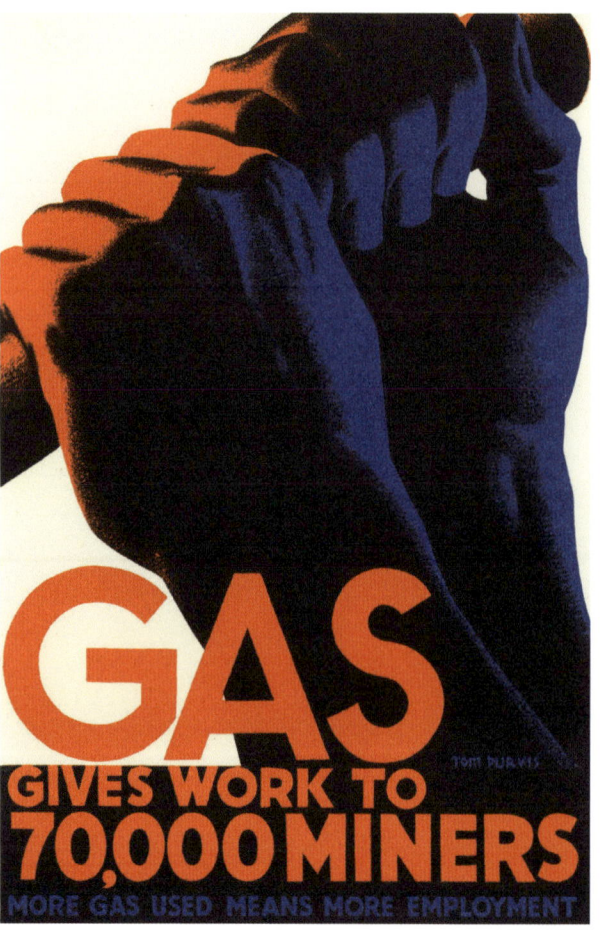

The Gas Light and Coke Company advertisements, *Commercial Art*, 1936

Penrose Annual, Vol. 39, 1937

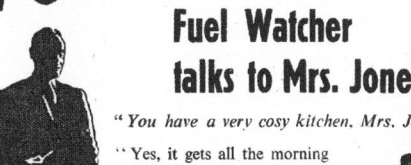

Ministry of Fuel and Power advertisement, *Housewife Magazine*, 1944

Ministry of Fuel and Power advertisement, *Housewife Magazine*, 1945

British Gas Council advertisement, 1940s

British Gas Council advertisement, *Art and Industry*, 1947

A Thousand and One Uses for Gas. Combining business and social activism she worked tirelessly for the BCGA until the mid-thirties, campaigning for the woman's point of view in the usage of gas and gas appliances. Having successfully linked gas usage to patriotism in WWI, BCGA went on to give gas brownie points by linking it, in its advertising, to public health, 'scientific housewifery' and social reform, in the inter-war years.

The BCGA's first major exhibition appearance, after the end of WWI, was at the British Empire Exhibition in 1924, in which it was able to demonstrate the use of gas for both industry and the home with a display said to have cost around £75,000 [over one and a quarter million pounds in today's money]. Sir Lawrence Weaver, responsible for the look of the whole exhibition, rated the gas industry display, 'The Seven Ages of Woman', as the 'best co-ordinated effort'. The BCGA had brought in yet another formidable woman to advise them for this, Mrs. Ethel M. Wood of the advertising agency Samson Clark.

The BCGA was also to make use of commercial artists of note for its advertising, such as the challenging cubist stylist Clive Gardiner. But its early commissioning of Septimus Scott proved less noteworthy. He had been briefed to devise an emblem representing 'gas', but his grandiose 'The Spirit of Coal', produced in the early 1920s, failed to catch the public's imagination. However, things were to change for the better with the arrival of Mr. Therm. By the late 20s the 'therm' had become the statutory standard measure for gas production and sale, and Eric Fraser [said never to have put pencil to paper without being commissioned] was asked to produce a character that looked like a gas flame and that hopefully would be taken up as an emblem for the industry. Fraser's 'Mr. Therm' arrived around 1931, and was to hang around for some 30 years, such was his popularity.

Anne Glendenning recorded in 'Demons of Domesticity' –

Mr. Therm Enamel badge

> 'Within months of his first appearance Mr. Therm's flat schematic face, haloed head and stylised limbs appeared on hoardings, buses, trade exhibitions, posters and in showroom windows.'

He also appeared on a flood of allied merchandising – playing cards, children's toys, badges and booklets – barely anything emerging from the activities of the BCGA was produced without the sprightly figure of Mr. Therm. Possibly the most absurd use of his character was the Gas Light and Coke company's Therm Band with its musicians all outfitted as Mr. Therm. *Display*, in 1934, recorded that 'this amusing little fellow is a great favourite with the public'; and an article in *Art and Industry*, in 1937, writing of Fraser's work declared –

British Commercial Gas Association advertisement, *Picture Post*, 1945

'Fraser created our beloved Mr. Therm; that in itself ought to be enough to endear him to us.'

Fraser, himself, is said to have been thoroughly dissatisfied with the five guineas he received [although later a further 25 guineas was proffered]; and miffed when Mr. Therm was later drawn by what he considered hacks at the London Press Exchange. The 'hacks' were, however, said to have got much fun out of thinking up new settings for Mr. Therm. Mr. Therm morphed into the wise counsellor for gas users, as when the industry became concerned as to the amount of maintenance required by gas cookers. Mr. Therm coaxed the housewife along –

'Your cooker's always good as new with just a little help from you.'

Mr. Therm was not the only publicity success for the industry in the 1930s as the BCGA were pioneers in the use of documentary film to improve its image. These films did not directly 'sell' gas but covered a variety of social problems that were, supposedly, to imply the industry's general concern for and involvement in social improvement. The BCGA commissioned John Grierson's sister Ruby to produce *Housing Problems*, the first of several such films, and took some of Grierson's young documentary apostles on to its staff for further productions.

The 30s also saw the industry use architects in its publicity, not only showing off with its modernistic showrooms, as when

George Grey Wornum [famed for designing the RIBA building] was commissioned for the Leytonstone one, but actually when it commissioned Maxwell Fry to design a flat development – Kensal House – to show off how gas could run homes.

And it was in 1934 that the gas industry set up the Women's Gas Council [WGC], to act as a pressure group, mirroring, to an extent, the already established Electrical Association for Women. One, Kathleen Halpin, was appointed its secretary and she was soon touring the country helping to set up local branches. The WGC did not consider itself as a 'selling' branch of the industry so much as an educational and advisory body – running courses, issuing a magazine, and acting as the voice of the housewife user. Its success in these activities, however, provided unintentional public relations for the industry, accompanied, presumably, by an upping of sales. Nor was the WGC overtly 'feminist', stridently attempting to release women from household chores for more worthy endeavours; but it, nevertheless, worked, in a low key way, for the improvement of the conditions of women.

After WWII, poor Mr. Therm was retired, or rather thrust aside, when, in the 1960s natural gas arrived. The London Press Exchange was retired along with Mr. Therm, and Colman, Prentis & Varley were retained to give gas a new image, with the industry's unexpected revival. CPV were totally resistant to the cute charm of Mr. Therm and, indeed, found him irritating with his 'annoying wide smile and bright-eyed cheeriness'. 'Speed' became the key word in gas advertising, yet a degree of whimsy was retained with the connotation of such adjectives as 'whizzy' and the like.

High Speed Gas advertisement, *Ideal Home*, 1960s

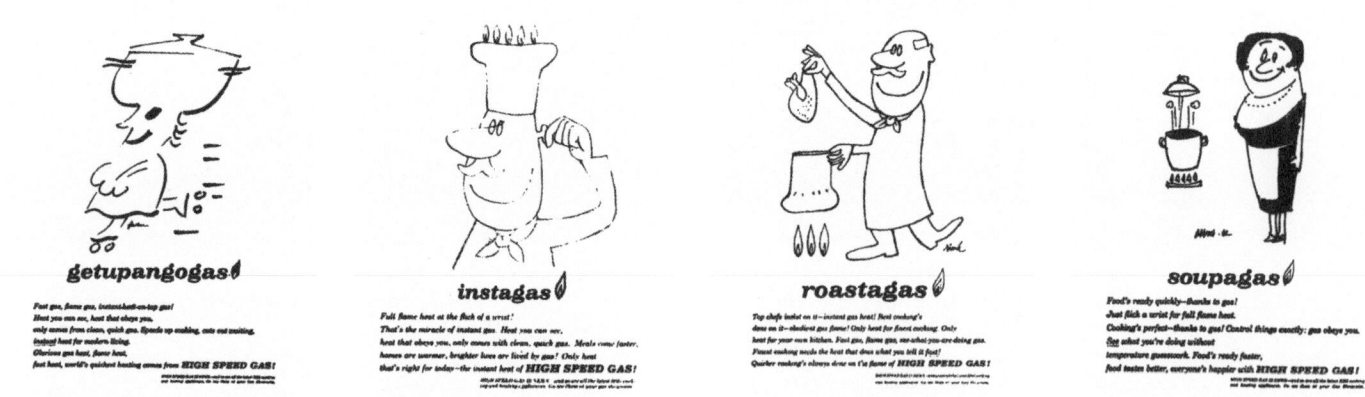

High Speed Gas advertisement, *Modern Publicity*, 1962/3

A typical advertisement in *Ideal Home* in 1962 managed to include the positives of gas, climaxing with the tag 'High Speed Gas' –

> *Glorious gas heat – rooms warm faster*
> *Obedient gas heat – never ever wasted!*
> *Heat when you want it.*
> *Heat in a jiffy. Fireside cosiness and warmth on tap.*
> *Faster, cleaner, easier, cosier – gas heats the world's most Comfortable homes! For one room warmth or central heating the quickest way is HIGH SPEED GAS!*

With gas nationalisation in the 1940s the Gas Council had become responsible for the industry's advertising and publicity and this continued into the 1970s, the period covered by this book.

Although electricity entered the domestic market slowly and later than gas, it was no slouch in being an active advertiser and publicity machine from the start. The Electricity Development Association [EDA] was established in 1919, and served as the industry's marketing and selling arm, much as the BCGA was to do for gas. As the BCGA had to battle the popular concept of gas being smelly, dirty and dangerous, so the EDA had to challenge people's fear of electricity, particularly as it could neither be seen nor heard. The EDA had the further problem with electricity being more expensive than gas and, until the National Grid was started via

Electrical Development Association leaflet, 1930s

General Electric Company advertisement, *The Home Magazine*, 1925

GREAT EXHIBITION · 1851

PHILIPS ELECTRICAL LTD

RADIO & TELEVISION RECEIVERS · TUNGSTEN, FLUORESCENT, BLENDED & DISCHARGE LAMPS & LIGHTING EQUIPMENT · 'PHILISHAVE' ELECTRIC DRY SHAVERS · CYCLE DYNAMO LIGHTING SETS · 'PHOTOFLUX' FLASH BULBS · HIGH-FREQUENCY HEATING GENERATORS · X-RAY EQUIPMENT FOR ALL PURPOSES · ELECTRO-MEDICAL APPARATUS · ARC & RESISTANCE WELDING PLANT & ELECTRODES · ELECTRONIC MEASURING INSTRUMENTS · MAGNETIC FILTERS · BATTERY CHARGERS & RECTIFIERS · SOUND AMPLIFYING INSTALLATIONS · CINEMA PROJECTORS · RECORDING APPARATUS · FINE WIRE & DIAMOND DIES

A page of history turns, and Hyde Park and Magic Lanterns give way to the South Bank and Television.

In the century between, nothing has done more to alter our way of life than the increased knowledge of electricity and its applications. And in the acquisition of that knowledge no organisation has played a more distinguished part than Philips, pioneers for over fifty years in all branches of electrical research and manufacture.

PHILIPS ELECTRICAL LTD · CENTURY HOUSE
SHAFTESBURY AVENUE · LONDON · W.C.2

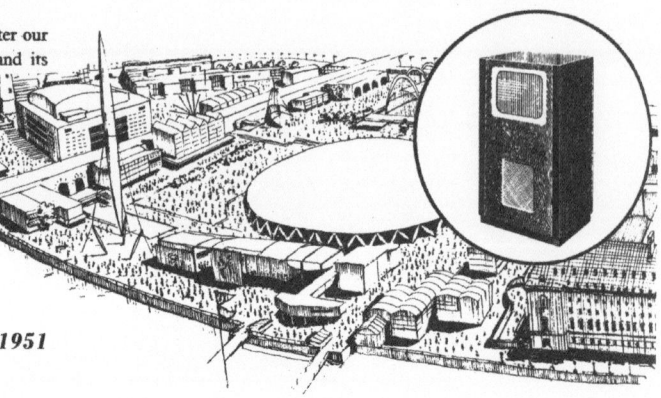

FESTIVAL OF BRITAIN · 1951

Philips advertisement, *Illustrated London News*, 1951

English Electric advertisement, *Courier Magazine*, January 1952

Central Electricity Generating Board advertisement, *The Listener*, 1961

the Electricity Act of 1926, supply was very unevenly spread across the country, and remained patchy until the grid was completed. The EDA, like the BCGA, began to take stands at exhibitions and to set up showrooms, but was rather quicker to appreciate the advantages of press and hoarding publicity and advertising.

The EDA was courageous in head-on snags and prejudices surrounding its product, but tended, from the start, to emphasise the scientific research underlying the industry and thereby to tie the industry to the future, in spite of the fact that by doing so it was encouraging a demand that could not be met, either by supply or appliances available. Early EDA tags ran along the lines – 'Science's greatest gift to the world – Electricity', 'For Health's Sake – use Electricity', 'Electricity provides the modern housewife with the perfect servant – clean, silent, economical' and 'To electricity belongs the Present and the Future'. The EDA implied that you were lagging behind if you were not up there with the 'goers', if you still relied on coal and gas.

This approach served well in the thirties but had to be modified during the years of the second world war as the industry turned to munitions and as electricity became vital to the war effort. Then 'patriotism' became EDA's banner, encouraging the populous to be loyal to electricity but to be careful in its usage for the nation's survival –

'Electricity cuts the metal and welds the structures, assembles the parts and transports the completed job. In

every stage of war production electricity is the driving force. That is why WE MUST SAVE FUEL TODAY.'

EDA's hands were similarly tied in the immediate post-war years whilst power plants were being restored and extended. Nevertheless, many manufacturers of electrically driven domestic appliances were beginning to pour out models that contained state of the art technology, an understanding of which they had gained by their wartime government funded munitions work. The EDA was obliged to shift from encouraging the unrestricted use of electricity to again urging economy. This they did by a two-pronged advertising campaign, on the one hand urging sparing use in what was termed 'peak' hours [judged to be between 7.45 and 9am and 4.30 to 6pm]; and the use of storage units. The appeal was blunt and direct – 'Use electricity in off-peak periods and avoid cuts'.

From the mid-50s and into the 60s the EDA was able to return to the positive promotion of electricity, using both traditional media along with film and television. It was still active in showing at exhibitions, in 1957 recorded as having displays in some 32. All this effort was further aided by the bringing in of the Clean Air Act in 1956. 'Plug in to electric living' was to be a common tag for the 60s and the EDA gained sufficient confidence to even put out the odd advertisement without an electric appliance in sight, as with a saucy view of a young bikinied girl splayed out in her garden –

'A very small price for such a large slice of freedom, and a right to a place in the sun.'

Electrical Development Association advertisement, *Ideal Home*, 1961

With electricity supply catching up with demand the EDA was also able to stress the service aspects of the industry – well tested appliances, impartial advice, wide choice, generous HP terms, professional installation and good aftersales service.

The electrical industry, as with the gas, was originally considered a man's realm. The EDA turned down the idea of a women's organisation to further its cause and it was the Women's Engineering Society which was to run with the possibility. The Electrical Association for Women [EAW] was formed in 1924 with Caroline Haslett as Director. Its aim was not so much the selling of electricity or electrical appliances but, in this case, directly, the empowerment of women –

> *'…women free from drudgery which ate up energy and sapped interest; of women free from the curse of the Serpent laid upon them; to eat bread by the sweat of the brow.'*

The slogan was 'Emancipation from drudgery', and soon branches of the EAW were springing up across the country frequently involving the local lady of the manor or such like – titles were abundant. One example of its early output will catch the flavour –

> *'Women appear to have electrical homes for different reasons. The Dowager Lady Swaythling rejoices that 'there is not a cold corner in her house' since she brought electricity into it. Lady Mount Temple delights in the beauty of light in the right place. Lady Belhaven & Stenton congratulates herself that she has revolutionised the labour of a big country house. Mrs. Herbert Morrison is glad of electricity, because it gives her time for public work.'*

Such like makes distasteful reading to the liberated woman of today, although it was no doubt politically astute to involve such 'influential' women at its start. In fact the EAW came to be a very down-to-earth affair, helping women to be competent and confident in their use of electrical appliances and coming to influence government policy on the workings of the supply authorities and on housing matters, as well as more directly influencing architects and builders. It set up electrical housecraft courses in schools and colleges, established a diploma for demonstrators of electrical equipment, ran its own school in Regent Street, laid on exhibitions and conferences and had an outpouring of pamphlets and leaflets. By such energy and enthusiasm the EAW eventually won over the EDA and had government departments sitting up and taking notice. The EAW saw the spread of electricity as part-and-parcel of the emancipation of women, and, further, of human progress. It had no intention of <u>selling</u> electric power or electric appliances, but by its educational and empowering activities it clearly must have incidentally had a major impact on sales, become, inadvertently, a considerable publicity arm for the industry. Eventually it was to be part-funded by the Central Electricity Generating Board and continued its evangelism through to the mid 1980s, being dissolved in 1986, when the industry returned to consisting of competitive companies.

THE GAS AND ELECTRICITY INDUSTRIES

EDA advertisement, *Ideal Home*, 1965

The Gas Council advertisement, *Homemaker*, 1966

COOKING

Although both gas and electric cookers were being demonstrated in the 19th century, they were slow to find a domestic market. Even when the gas industry sought other outlets for its product than lighting, with electricity looming competitively on the horizon, it was the commercial kitchens of hotels, restaurants and such which were the primary targets of the industry's marketing.

The main advantage of gas cooking over electricity was its relative cheapness, and much was made of this in advertising over the years. A typical early 1920s advertisement for the Falkirk Iron Company's 'Smoothtop' gas range of cookers spelt out how a meal of Irish stew, potatoes, fruit and custard and coffee for nine people could only cost one and a quarter pennies in gas. Right through to post-WWII Mr. Therm continued to stress how inexpensive cooking by gas might be with the New World No.1430

G.E.C. Kettle advertisement, *Woman's Realm* (detail), 1958

Refrigerator Booklet, 1930s

Gas Cooker – 'which cuts your gas bills by 20%'. New World were still using price as its selling point in 1968 with its New World 45 being hyped for 'little-budget big families'.

Whilst gas marketing stressed cheapness, electric cooker manufacturers were playing the cleanliness and ease of cleaning card. Belling, whose 'Modernette' had come onto the market in 1919, continually plugged the ease of cleaning electric plates and its oven which was merely –

'...a plain enamelled 'box' containing nothing except shelves and runners. Extremely easy to clean.'

As with gas and price, electric cookers maintained this line of argument through the period covered by this book. A Hotpoint advertisement of 1968 extolling cleaning as 'the big big plus' of its Hi-Speed Electric cookers –

'The whole hob hinges up to clean the drip tray and underside of the hob. The main oven door and glass

R&A Main gas cooker advertisement, c1920s

door lift off. Oven top, bottom and sides slide out – and are so sized that they fit into a normal sink. No cooker cleans easier than Hi-Speed Electric.'

A major snag with early cookers, whether run on gas or by electricity, was the control of temperature, and when the various regulatory gismos came in from the late 1920s onwards, much was made of this advance in advertisements. Radiation's 'New World' had its 'Regulo', R&A Main its 'Mainstat', the Parkinson Stone Co. its 'Ajusto', Belling its 'Tem-set', Moffat its 'Thermo-matic', and so on. Most of the advertising linked automatic regulation to freeing up the housewife, as 'New World' taking full-pages for its advertisements with sketches of elegantly clad women –

'Whilst the dinner is cooking itself you can shop, call on friends, or do what you wish.'

and –

'My dinner is cooking at home now, while I am out shopping. At quarter to 12 I put in fish, joint, vegetables and a sweet. At one o'clock I shall go back home and there they will be, ready to serve – beautifully cooked too.'

The introduction of temperature regulation was soon to be followed, in the 1930s, by the arrival of the oven glass door – the Vulcan Stoves 'Armourplate', the Belling 'Double Glass' etc. Belling spelt out its advantage –

Vulcan Stoves advertisement, *Home and Garden*, 1936

Belling cookers advertisement, *Woman's Journal*, 1935

Ritemp Cookery Book, c1940s

Frigidaire advertisement, *Milady Magazine*, 1952

New World gas cookers leaflet, 1960s

'You've often looked into your present oven to see how the pastry is 'getting on', haven't you? – hoping to goodness that the cold air won't make everything heavy. Now you can see your pastry turning a lovely golden brown before your eyes without opening the door.'

Other attributes to the cooker, hyped up as they were introduced, were the placing and size of the grill, the facilities for keeping plates and dishes warm, storage compartments, fold-down tops, the placing of the control panel and the size of the oven. American models were particularly vociferous in their advertising about size as with Frigidaire's post-war electric range advertised for the British market – 'a range to make you a very proud and envied woman indeed' –

*'Giant Full-Width Oven
The biggest oven you'll ever need…gives even heat all over…heavily insulated on all six sides…costs no more to use.'*

Over the years the cooker was continuously refined in design, each addition exploited in publicity, to the extent that Creda was taking a full page advertisement in the 1960s in *The Queen* in order to cover some dozen or so advantages of its latest model – quick discs, sealed to hob for easy cleaning, fast heating, easy working height, less stooping, sealed inner glass door, large warming drawer, automatic oven, clock face timer, high splash plate, light click-close Sealatch and family size grill. As with the Frigidaire and other models advertisements frequently suggested that any housewife possessing such a model would 'let the Joneses keep up with you!' appealing to pride - in one's competence to handle such technically remarkable machines, and competitiveness – in that you would be ahead of the field.

Gas and electric showrooms spread across the country with the latest cookers on show, often displayed so that one was obliged to pass them on the way to pay bills. And many cooker manufacturers supplied cookbooks as Utilo's 'hints for using the Utilo electric cooker together with sixty-three recipes'. Some firms even offered 'freebies' as baits, such as Vulcan Stoves' four Pyrex dishes, albeit there was little evidence that these improved sales. For the period covered by this book the electric cooker never caught up in popularity with the gas, in spite of considerable advertising budgets. One estimate showed only 6% of homes using an electric cooker in 1935, rising to 22% in 1955, but still below half even into the 1980s.

As with most powered domestic appliances the Americans were well ahead when it came to refrigeration, motivated, it is claimed, by more extremes of weather and a sparser population with shops not easily accessible. Although both Frigidaire and Kelvinator were exporting to Britain in the 1920s, and the Swedish firm, Electrolux, was manufacturing its refrigerators here by 1927, refrigeration was somewhat slow to catch on. Pressed Steel's

Kelvinator advertisement, *Woman's Journal*, 1935

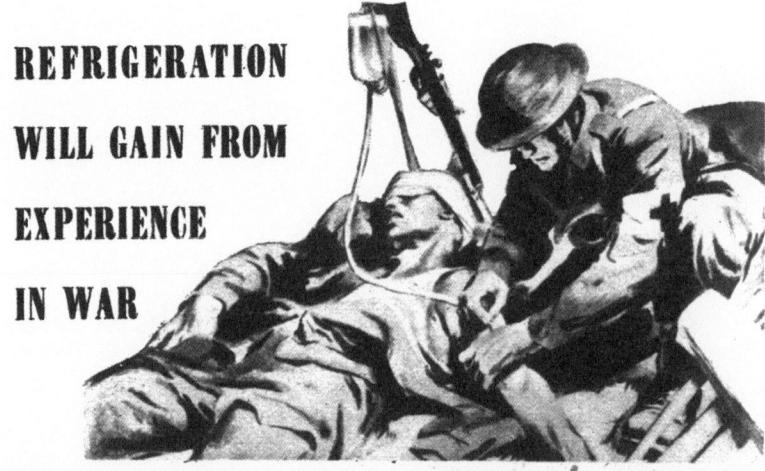

Prestcold advertisement, *Woman's Journal*, 1935

Prestcold advertisement, *Picture Post*, 1945

COOKING

English Electric advertisement, *Punch*, 1955

Electrolux advertisement, *Ideal Home*, 1968

'Prestcold' trying to keep up with the American invasion. By 1939 it was estimated that only 200,000 homes owned a refrigerator – the explosion was to come in the post-WWII years; by the 1960s the number had risen to some five million.

Early models were little more than wooden cabinets, some, like Electrolux, needing a cold water supply. But soon, certainly in the States, refrigerators grew in size and splendour, and, spawned from the car industry, came to be second only to the car in endowing social status on the owner.

The advertising of refrigerators was huge and soon the likes of Frigidaire and Kelvinator were adapting their techniques to the British market. An early Frigidaire advertisement, appearing in *Punch* in 1930, actually resorted to English whimsy both in its imagery and copy –

'How gracious these dews of Solace
That over my sense fall
At the clink of the ice in the tumbler
The boys bring up the hall.'

'The 'dews of Solace' are always on tap if you
are the lucky possessor of a Frigidaire.'

But Frigidaire couldn't resist its Americanism in the tail of the advertisement –

'In fact, now that a Frigidaire can be installed for so little, it's advisable to buy quickly, if one's social status is to remain in status quo.'

Although a number of angles were used in the advertising of refrigerators – hygiene, limited food wastage, a new branch of cooking [cold menus] and freshness – the main thrust seems to have been the size of a refrigerator's holding capacity and the smallness of the actual floor space it occupied. Prestcold, following the American lead, declared of one of its models – 'it holds so much more than any other refrigerator of equal price', and used the tags 'more space for less money' and 'greater in space – greater in grace'. The real battle of size began in the post-war period, each manufacturer leaping over each other as to how many cubic feet were enclosed; and further, how this space was divided – the relative size of the freezer compartment, the cleverness of the shelving, the divisions on the door.

The Americans were similarly ahead when it came to the myriad of small cooking utensils that came to be powered, as electric kettles, coffee percolators, mixers etc., the Brits only scoring with the toaster, which Crompton & Co. had produced as early as 1893, albeit the toast had to be turned by hand. Although the Americans had introduced the pop-up toaster by the mid-20s, the drop side toaster remained on the market alongside it for much of the inter-war period. By the post-WWII years many of the manufacturers of large kitchen appliances had added a toaster to their range, including Philips, Siemens, Braun and Moulinex, but it was the Morphy-Richards models that were to become market

Kenwood advertisement, *Punch*, 1953

leaders. With designers as Major Bill Russell [later of Russell Hobbs], the Morphy-Richards toaster had become automatic by 1956, and was able to be advertised as 'no fuss, no mess, no burning' –

> '...handsome to look at, easy to keep clean, it's the finest time and trouble saving aid you could find.'

And, indeed, for a time, the 'handsome' façade of many brands of toaster besported small works of art on their sides, as, for example, sheaves of corn, to make them look more attractive standing on the breakfast table.

The electric kettle, along with the toaster, were two of the earliest small electric appliances to be found in the kitchen, an electric kettle being exhibited in the 1890s in Chicago World Fair. The major practical problem with the early electric kettle was that it could boil dry and the concept of cut-out was only gradually devised. Although Morphy-Richards had a popular model on the market by the 1930s, it was two of the company's ex-employees, Russell and Hobbs, who produced the first British vapour controlled cut-out automatic kettle in 1955, along with the first automatic coffee percolator. Russell Hobbs, in its advertising, had its delighted housewives clapping their hands with 'Hooray! Just what I wanted for Xmas'; and its sophisticated 'women of reputation' entertaining their women friends effortlessly at coffee mornings, having already done the shopping – all without domestic help!

'Cut-out' became a key selling point along with the speed of heating water; an electric kettle of 1902 is recorded as taking 12 minutes to boil – one in the 1960s took one minute. Hotpoint, was one of many manufacturers to make much of speed when in 1965 it used Violet Carson [the much loved Ena Sharples of the television soap Coronation Street] in one of its advertisements –

> 'When I want to buy an electric kettle they said Hotpoint was the fastest – 85 seconds to boil a pint of water. Right, I said, I'll have one of those. 85 seconds is long enough for any woman to wait for her cup of tea. How much? 5 guineas. Right I said, wrap it up.'

The electric kettle morphed from a container with a bare heating element inside, to one with the heating element enclosed, to a jug shaped work of art, with even the likes of the design genius F.A. Porsche applying his imagination in the competition for the kettle to become a design icon. Whereas Violet Carson could boast of speed, other advertising made the purchase of a 'designed' electric kettle a symbol of avant garde-taste.

During the 20th century there was hardly an article lying about the kitchen to which someone didn't try to affix an electric motor, and the number of possibilities increased as the motor compacted. When it came to food processors [combining a number of gadgets together] the Americans were yet again ahead in the inter-war years with mixers, liquidisers, can openers and the like. But it was Kenwood, a company not established until 1947 that was to dominate the British post-war market, much aided along by its consultant designer Kenneth Grange. From the early 1950s the Kenwood Chef was the by-word when it came to food processors. An early Kenwood advertisement, in 1953, boasted the multi-skills of the machine –

> 'At the touch of a switch it mixes, minces, whips, creams, grinds, mashes, beats, peels, blends, purees and juices.'

And yet again there were happy housewives, 'proud possessors' of the machine, and smug husbands 'I can take a hint – I'm giving my wife a Kenwood Chef right away!' A 1962 Kenwood advertisement can only be read with incredulity by a 21st century woman –

> 'The Chef does everything but cook – that's what wives are for.'

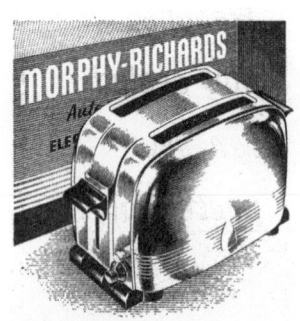

Toaster advertisement, *Punch*, 1954

COOKING

G.E.C. advertisement, *Woman's Realm*, 1958

Hotpoint advertisement, *Ideal Home*, 1965

CLEANING

Although many people still use the word 'hoover' when referring to an electric cleaner, and, indeed, Scrabble has embraced it, without its capital, as an acceptable common word, Hoover was not the first inventor of such a domestic appliance. The credit for this generally goes to an Englishman, one Cecil Booth, an engineer, who in 1901, it is claimed was the first to combine a power driven suction pump and dust collecting filter in one machine. He employed uniform clad men to demonstrate his machine, and wealthy hostesses are said to have held 'cleaner' tea parties where such a wonder would be demonstrated. Booth's Vacuum Cleaning Company came to be renamed, in 1926, GOBLIN [BVC] and Goblin was to become one of the major brands of electric cleaner at the budget end of the market in the interwar years.

Meanwhile, in the States, an asthmatic, J.M. Spangler, troubled by dust, was experimenting with what has derisorily been described as a broom and a pillow case. A Mr. W.H. Hoover, at that time a saddlemaker, came across Mr. Spangler's experiments, bought the rights, and the rest is history. The Hoover appeared on the British market in 1912, and a commercial battle commenced with Goblin, and with the Swedish import, Electrolux. Electrolux had enclosed the motor and fan in a metal cylinder – the canister model – which glided along the floor on metal skis. Gradually other companies joined the 'cleaner' competition, through to the 60s, including General Electric, Philips, Miele, Rowenta and AEG.

Unlike other powered domestic appliances, the cleaner was initially sold by door-to-door salesmen, able to demonstrate to the housewife on the spot. So key was the mobile salesman to Hoover that a large Hoover advertisement, as late as 1939, had no sight of the machine itself, but only the besuited, behatted salesman, along with the tag 'He stands for freedom from drudgery'.

Although some of the 'cleaner' advertising in the 1920s tended to focus on 'power', as Electrolux claiming its machine to be 'The World's Most Powerful Suction Cleaner', the main thrust of the advertising stressed the 'freedom' that was being offered to the housewife. 'Drudgery' was the most frequently occurring word, as with Hoover's 'does away with so much soul-destroying drudgery', and Vactric's 'I said Goodbye to Drudgery for 2/- a week' [the cleaner as with many domestic appliances, was available for hire as

Servis electric washers advertisement (detail), *Punch*, 1956

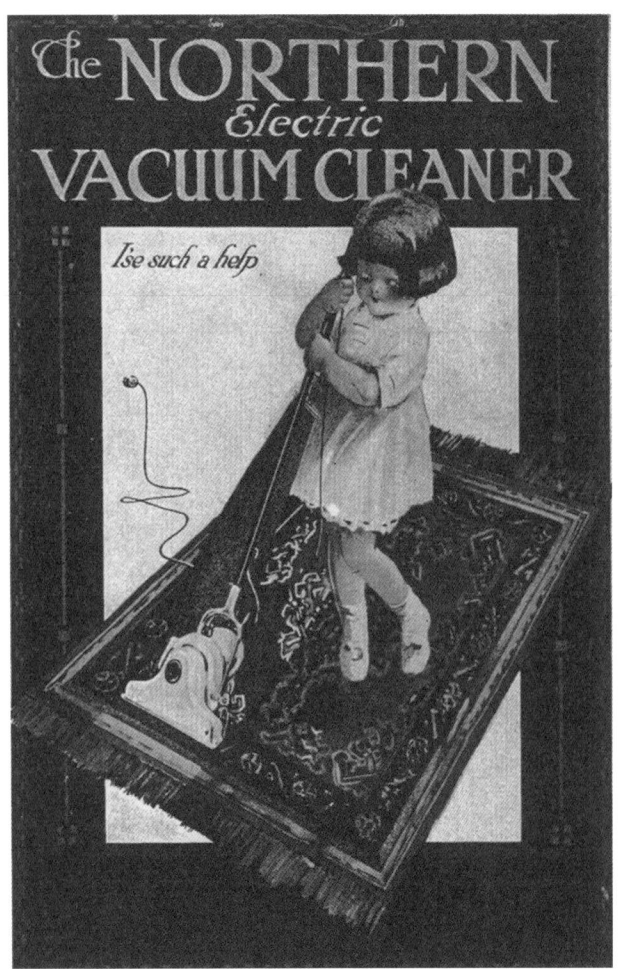

Northern Electric advertisement, *Commercial Art*, 1922

well as to be bought on hire purchase]. Electrolux was using much the same argument with its somewhat dramatic –

> 'Day after day, the same tedious task of home cleaning, tiring you out and aging you.'

And Hoover was carrying on with this anti-drudgery line into the post-WWII years, illustrating the sheer delight and relief of the housewife on opening her Xmas present –

> 'How excited and pleased she'll be at getting a Hoover.'

and

> 'Give her a Hoover – the gift she really wants.'

Really!! But then Hoover came up with its catch phrase used for hyping its cleaner that was to become so popular –

> 'It beats…as it sweeps…as it cleans.'

As with most post-WWI advertising, the images of cleaners became colourful, and the copy began to add additional advantages, not previously made much of, as Electrolux stressing the quietness of its machines – 'Thanks to this quietness you can always hear the postman knock'; and further Electrolux felt able to boast that one could do as many related activities with its two attachments as with the countless range offered by other manufacturers.

A 1965 Electrolux advertisement listed all the attributes

CLEANING

THE *Perfect* CHRISTMAS GIFT
—*freedom from Cleaning Drudgery*

A Merry Christmas and a Hoover New Year

The latest type of Hoover—at the pre-war price!

How excited and pleased she'll be at getting a Hoover Cleaner. Hours of back-aching drudgery saved every week for years to come, better health, greater happiness. It is the World's Best Cleaner! The latest streamlined models — with all modern refinements – are still available at pre-war prices. Ask your Authorised Hoover Dealer to give you a demonstration. There is a model for every size and type of home.

Prices from **£10.10.0 to £20.8.0** (*plus purchase tax*)

The HOOVER
REGISTERED TRADE MARK

It BEATS... *as it Sweeps... as it Cleans*

HOOVER LIMITED · PERIVALE · GREENFORD · MIDDLESEX

Hoover advertisement, *Country Life*, 1947

Give her a Hoover
—*the gift she really wants*

She deserves the best, doesn't she? So give her a Hoover Cleaner, the gift she really wants — the gift that goes on being remembered week after week, month after month, year after year — giving her freedom from hard back-aching drudgery.

But be sure you insist on a Hoover! That's the cleaner she wants because she knows it is the best. There is a model for every size and type of home. Prices from £10.10.0 to £21 (plus purchase tax). To ensure early delivery see your Authorised Hoover Dealer *now*.

The HOOVER
Rez. Trade Mark

It BEATS
... *as it sweeps ... as it cleans*

Hoover advertisement, *Home Notes*, 1948

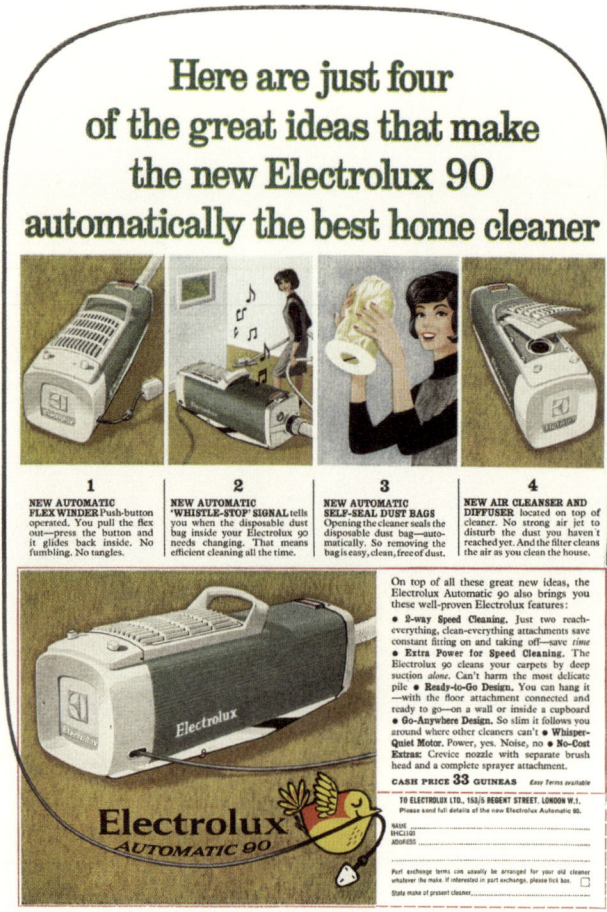

Electrolux advertisement, *Ideal Home*, 1965

that by then were to be expected of a cleaner – that it was slim and light, quiet, that it had a flex winder, that the dust bags were easy to handle [in the case of Electrolux the bags self-sealed as the canister was opened], and, a rarity it considered not to be found in other models – a 'whistle-stop signal' that told the user when the dust bag was full! Hotpoint was more pithy with 'it weighs less, costs less, cleans better' and spiced its advertisements with 'sex' as in the shape of a then young starlet, Shirley Anne Field, sitting on an exotic carpet, the cleaner perched on her left arm, not an apron in sight, but with a kind of suggestive ogle in her eyes hinting at how the time saved from drudgery might otherwise be spent!

When it came to washing, before the 19th century clothes tended only to be washed when absolutely necessary, even when water began to be piped to dwellings. By the end of the century most homes had their own water supply and a washday was set aside for the task of cleaning clothes and linen. The majority of people relied on a washtub to which was added hot water, a corrugated washboard, a dolly [or agitator] and a separate wringer, sometimes attached, sometimes standing free. Power applied to the cleaning of clothes and linen in the form of the washing machine was a relatively latecomer. Although, even before WWI manufacturers were experimenting by attaching an electric motor to a washtub, the commercial marketing of domestic washing machines in the UK only really began, to any extent, in the late 30s. Even then machines needed to be filled with water and drained, usually by a hose pipe attached to the kitchen sink; and each garment had to be put separately through a wringer attached to the outside of the machine,

Servis still having its wringer so attached through the 1950s. It is estimated that only 2% of households had a washing machine before 1947, and this had only risen to 25% by 1947. Most of these machines were loaded from the top and tended to have a cover that was hyped as adding additional kitchen surfacing – 'when not in use it will make a handy kitchen table'.

Of course the main selling point with washing machines was again labour saving, as in an IIMV advertisement in 1937 – 'without fuss, fatigue or laundry bills', or for the Co-operative Wholesale Society's 'Climax' – 'washing is no longer a nightmare'. With production on hold during the war years, post-war advertising began to spell out specific characteristics as the new machines coming on to the market advanced technically, becoming increasingly automated. Typical advertising were for English Elcctric's 'Liberator', with the tag – 'Set it – forget it'; and for Hoover's 'Keymatic' – 'Remember washday? Well... forget it'. A Bendix advertisement actually has a man making an appearance, albeit sitting in an armchair with a newspaper – 'From now on, even I can do the washing'.

Bendix, an American product manufactured in England under licence to Fisher & Ludlow, came on to the market around 1946 and led the field when it came to automation –

> '...*no wet floors, no scrubbing, no wringing, no clouds of steam – you just set it and forget it.*'

Tagging up the advantages of its latest model –

Hotpoint advertisement, *Ideal Home*, 1965

Bendix advertisement, *Ideal Home*, 1949

Climax advertisement, *Picture Post*, 1939

Servis Electric Washers advertisement, *Punch*, 1956

TWO IRONS IN ONE!
Damps while it presses,
irons dry if required!

THE SILEX STEAM IRON gives an improved finish to all ironing. It glides on a cushion of steam that banishes all wrinkles. Damping is unnecessary because it damps while it presses. Any degree of heat between low and high is obtainable and thermostatically maintained. A flick of a lever, and the "Silex" is a *dry* iron. Two irons in one, but no heavier than an ordinary iron! Guaranteed for 12 months. Price 59/6d.

THE SILEX ELECTRIC HEAT-CONTROLLED Steam Iron
Silex Household Products Ltd., 9-21 Cutler St., London, E.1.

Silex advertisement, *Housewife*, 1947

'…soaks, washes, rinses three times, damp dries, drains itself, switches off ALL BY ITSELF.'

Issues that became matters for competitiveness in advertising were the load capacity, the aftersales service, and the number of washing and drying programmes available; and, with the introduction of detergents needing less water, how small the tub could be for the same load.

It was not really until the 1960s that washing machines became cheap enough for the run-of-the-mill household to buy; and it was well into the 1970s before the market became really competitive with Italy's Zanussi, Holland's Philips and Germany's Bosch all becoming major players. By 1980 some 77% of United Kingdom households possessed a washing machine – the explosion had all been in the post-war years.

After the washing and drying came the ironing. Ironing, until the late 19th century was done with a block of metal with a handle heated over a fire, or sometimes hollow, filled with embers, bees-waxed or candle-greased sufficiently to slide over the material to be pressed. The first electric iron is credited to France sometime in the 1880s, but this was soon to be followed by similar inventions in the States and then in England. Early attempts to market gas irons seem to have been overtaken by the ease of harnessing electricity to the pressing process. The early electric irons were cordless and heated on electrically heated pads, a method soon found wanting as the iron lost heat too quickly. Eventually a cord was attached which, initially, was fed from a light socket. Although by the turn of the century both G.E.C. and Crompton's had electric irons on the market they were not really adopted to any extent in Britain until after WWI; and by the late 20s and into the 30s the thermostat had been introduced. A 1939 British Electric Domestic Appliance Company advertisement for its Mary Ann doubleway iron, was able to offer a nine foot cord and a heat control dial in 'lovely shades of cream, pastel green or powder blue', and, as with so many other domestic appliances, assured the reader 'She'd love an iron like this for Christmas'. Irons using steam and spray did not come on to the market until after WWII; both Silex and Hoover were already advertising this advance in the late 40s and early 50s, Silex declaring it really thereby was offering with its appliance two irons in one – 'Damps while it presses, irons dry if required'. But it was the Morphy-Richards 'safety electric iron' that came to dominate the British market in the post-war years, so popular that the company was able to claim it 'famous all over the world'. Its streamlined design and variously coloured body was to

Gas iron advertisement, *Commercial Art*, 1931

British Electric Domestic Appliance's advertisement, *Picture Post*, 1939

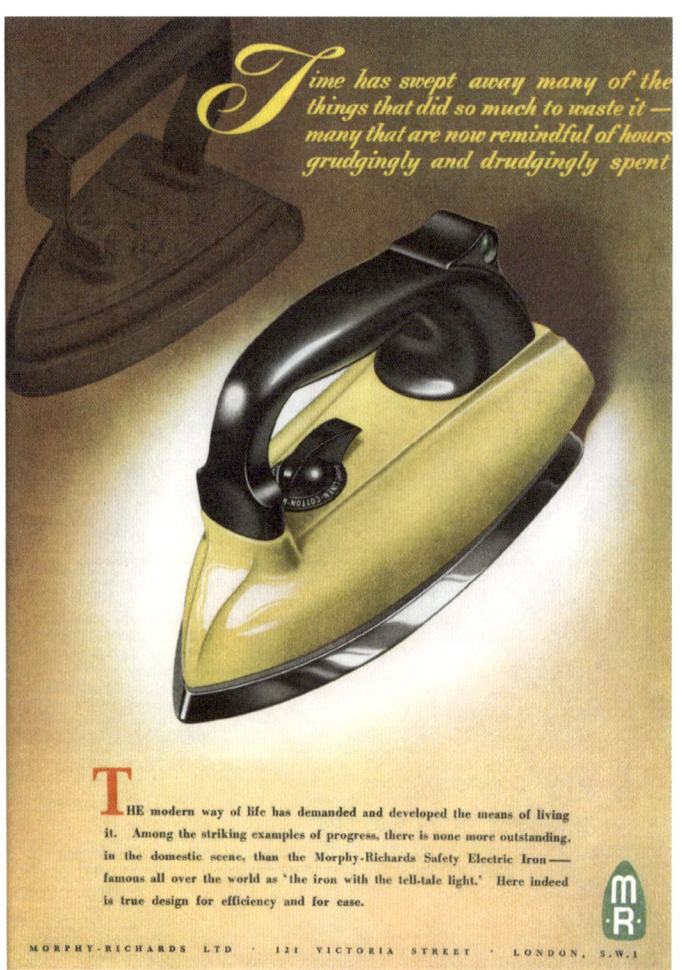

Morphy-Richards advertisement, *Design in the Festival*, 1951

become one of the icons of domestic appliances – when one thought 'iron', one thought Morphy-Richards.

Early attempts to market gas irons seem to have been overtaken by the ease and popularity of harnessing electricity to the process of pressing.

Of all the large white goods concerned with getting things clean, the dishwasher was the last to arrive, although one had been put on show in New York as early as 1910, and a model arrived on the British scene in 1937; as with the washing machine, the dishwasher wasn't widely available until the 1960s. Again the States were to the fore, General Electric, Hotpoint, Westinghouse and Frigidaire, amongst others, all offering domestic sized machines. And again, as with the washing machine, the early dishwashers had to be attached by pipes to a sink. As far as the British market was concerned they tended to be considered unnecessary unless there was a very large household much given to entertaining.

Even as late as 1965 Colston were offering a small model that stood on a surface near the sink with pipes to the tap and the drain. Yet in the very same year Kenwood launched a fully automated machine with 'rotosurge action, triple rinsing, able to take six place settings, fitting into any size kitchen', and 'half the price of other machines'. The general direction of early washing up machines advertising besides reducing drudgery, included such advantages as the protection of one's hands – 'they need never touch the water', as hygiene – 'no germ-laden dish mops and tea towels', and the thoroughness of the clean [egg being frequently quoted as difficult to remove by hand, easy by machine].

Kenwood advertisement, *Ideal Home*, 1965

LIGHTING

Although by the mid-19th century there were hundreds of companies making and selling gas, it wasn't really until the gas mantel had been invented in the 1880s [improving the safety of the flame], that gas became the main power for lighting the home. But while this was happening the likes of Rookes Crompton, Joseph Swan and Thomas Edison were experimenting with electricity generating and lighting systems that were eventually to bring electricity to the home to replace gas, as far as lighting was concerned. By 1883, Edison and Swan, originally at loggerheads over patent copyright, had merged together to form the Edison & Swan United Electric Light Co. to exploit what had largely been Swan's design for the electric light bulb i.e. placing an electric filament within a glass bulb.

Although electricity as a light source was superior to gas in that it was clean, quiet and did not give out a smell, it proved

Early 20th century 'as if by magic' electric lamp advertising

Osram Stamp, 1922

expensive, and, of course, nearly entirely dependent on the growth of the electricity supply industry and what was to become the National Grid. When it came to lighting, by the early 1930s Crompton and Edison & Swan had been joined by Philips, in the Netherlands, by Thorn [with Atlas lamps], by Germany's AEG [with Osram Lamps] and by the American General Electric Company's Mazda lamps, the last to become a major player on the British market.

What was referred to as a lamp in all the related advertising was what we know as a light bulb, and it was these that were mainly featured in advertisements rather than the changing fashions in light fittings. Advertising became highly competitive and yet there was little to choose between the main contenders, and it was perhaps this that stretched manufacturers' imagination in trying to make their bulb stand out from the others. Early competitiveness between gas and electric lighting had to be replaced by more subtle messages, when one bulb manufacturer was pitted against another. The actual power of the bulb was an obvious factor, with one manufacturer

Edison Swan advertisement, *Punch*, 1947

leap frogging over another in claims, such as Crompton's declaring that its bulb gave 'one fifth more light than others'.

Most companies, at one time or another, stressed the importance of good lighting to protect eyesight, as Ediswan [which had become Royal Ediswan on receiving the Royal Warrant] making much of the elimination of eye-strain and the avoidance of headaches –

'If that lamp were lower down
You would not need to peer and frown.'

and

'Be light-wise! See that every lamp in your home is of the right type, the right wattage, and is placed in the right position.'

Osram, from the start, had linked its bulbs to mental health as 'light up and smile', and 'good light cheers'; and Siemens was perhaps touching on this aspect with its 'Siemen's electric lamps for brighter happier homes'. The cheerfulness of lighting became even more important in wartime, with blackout regulations, to which was added the patriotism of the particular manufacturer in its contribution to the war effort. Osram was to the fore with variations of 'your favourite lamps are helping to bring victory'; whilst Mazda joined in with its 'victory through light', and Royal Ediswan with 'Let's see a brighter future'. Most companies made much of the need to save on lighting to contribute to help on the home front, some actually resorting to humour to get their message across. Some bright spark, presumably at an advertising agency twigging that the 'Ph' of Philips was pronounced F came up with –

To save electricity	*To save electricity*
Phervid	*Phamous*
Phamilies	*Phinanciers*
Phit	*Phit*
Philips	*Philips*

and more such whimsy, suitably illustrated with cartoon figures.

Two developments in lighting in the late 1940s that brought specific advertising campaigns were the arrival of

Philips advertisement, *Picture Post*, 1942

Osram advertisement, 1944

Crompton advertisement, *Picture Post*, 1945

Atlas advertisement, *Picture Post*, 1945

Osram Lamp packaging, 1948

Philips poster, original artwork, 1949

Osram advertisement, designed by *Ashley Havinden*, 1949

Crompton advertisement, *Festival of Britain South Bank Catalogue*, 1951

Osram advertisements, 1950s

fluorescent lights and the design of the Anglepoise. Edison had actually patented a fluorescent lamp as early as 1907 but did not take it further. In the 1930s the American General Electric Company took up the challenge of fluorescence having bought up most of the relevant patents, and extended its use during the war. By the 1950s it was estimated that more light was being produced in the United States by fluorescent than by incandescent lamps, but presumably that would have included commercial and industrial as well as domestic use. The advantages advanced for the fluorescent lamp was that it produced a stronger and longer lasting light with less heat and glare; what was omitted was that it contained hazardous mercury and was more expensive to run, and would eventually become an environmental issue. Nevertheless it came to dominate the American market and was advertised both there and in Britain for its efficiency, and, indeed, as an aspect of interior design.

AEG took this latter line with its launch of the Mazda Netaline in the 1960s –

> 'Elegant – it's a beautifully designed fitting in a choice of yellow, red, blue or lilac.'

and

> 'If good design belongs in your home, so does the Mazda Netaline.'

And still the 'power' card was being played, as it had been in the 1920s –

Mazda advertisement, *House Beautiful*, 1964

LIGHTING

'The Mazda 40-watt warm white tube gives twice the light of an ordinary 100-watt bulb.'

Anglepoise had been conceived by the British car designer George Carwardine in 1932, whilst he was working on vehicle suspension systems. He began to manufacture and sell the lamps himself but finding the commercialisation of his idea too big to handle, he agreed to licence it to the Terry Spring Company of Redditch. Originally the lamp had been meant for workshops but Carwardine produced a domestic version in 1934. Terry's gave it considerable publicity, and even when war broke out promoted it as the 'ideal blackout lamp'. The design was to be copied by other manufacturers so 'anglepoise' has become as nearly a generic term as 'hoover'. Terry's tags for Anglepoise was 'just a touch' – for ease of adjustment, and '1001 angles' –

'That's the beauty of this wonderful lamp – you can alter its angles by the gentle finger touch for your reading, writing, sewing – for anything needing a perfect light.'

By the 1960s it had become a design icon, an ornamental asset –

'Get it for around a five-pound note, and in pace-setting white or red or yellow or green or cream or play-it-safe black.'

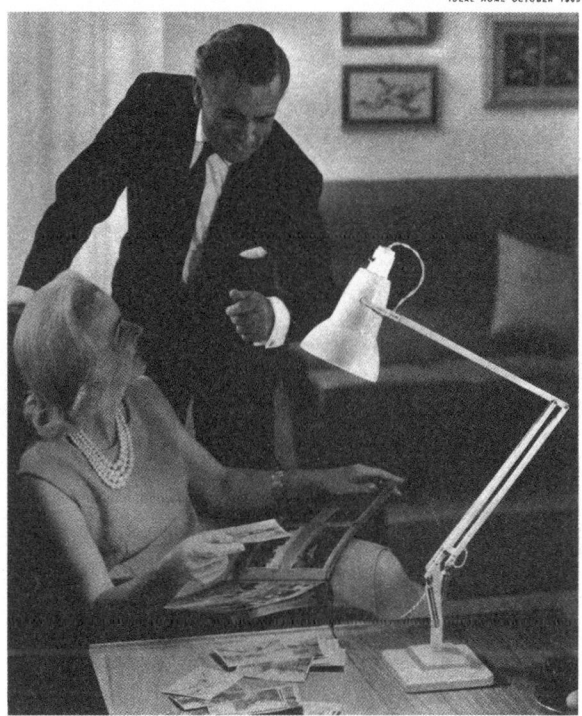

Anglepoise advertisement, *Ideal Home*, 1965

HEATING

Although both gas and electric fires were on the market before around the turn of the century, it has been estimated that some 75% of the population was still heating its main living room with coal, coke or anthracite right up to WWII. Sociologists and anthropologists would have it that there was something considered mystical about an open fire, the heart of the home, a kind of altar with a mantelpiece upon which were placed the most valued objects, as if the hearth gods seeing them would shower the house with good luck.

By the turn of the century it had come to be known that electric lights gave out more heat than light, and, building on this, one H.J. Dowsing devised an electric fire consisting of two extra large light bulbs placed vertically together. This early electric fire was manufactured by Crompton & Co. and it was an apprentice of that firm, Charles Reginald Belling, who, on leaving the firm, set up on his own in 1912, and made the breakthrough by using coiled wires for his first electric fire. This retained the functions of an open grate by having a trivet which could be let down to boil a kettle, and also a mechanism for making toast.

So strong was the pull of the open hearth with its homely flames, that soon after, Berry, to become a major competitor to Belling, devised the Magicoal Electric Fire, which, by 1920, not only had fake glowing coal [or fake logs], but flickered, as did a real flame. Berry, in his turn, spawned an apprentice who was to become a rival – Brett Colbran. Belling, Berry, Brett Colbran, along with Ferranti, Sun Electric, Cannon, Jackson and Creda, were to become the main manufacturers when it came to electric fires in the inter-war years [Colbran producing both gas and electric ones]. Electric fires, like much furniture at the time, were given names which, presumably, it was thought would make them more attractive to the market as Belling's 'Adam' and 'Mediaeval'; whilst the name of some of Berry's fires carried the name of their founder, however ridiculous the conjunction turned out to be, as 'Joyberry'. Ferranti's juxtapositions were even more awkward – as 'Glowera' and 'Flamera'.

Belling wrote his own advertising material, waxing lyrical about his products –

Berry's Magicoal advertisement, *Ideal Home (detail)*, 1951

British Commercial Gas Association advertisement, *Punch*, 1921

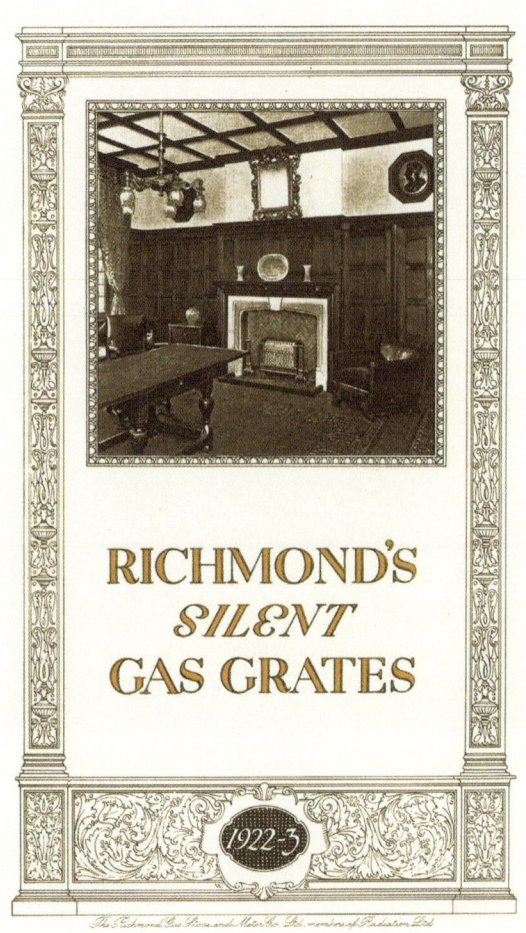

Radiation Ltd, Richmond advertisement, 1922–3

> '...so welcome to the unexpected guest as it becomes one mass of glowing heat a few moments after switching on. In nickel, brass or copper finish, with polished relief, the heater has a handsome appearance and is absolutely without smell and perfectly free from dust and dirt, it is most eminently suitable for the most elegant and daintily furnished home.'

Nor was the gas industry a slouch when it came to marketing its fires. The Commercial Gas Association, by the 1920s, was taking whole page advertisements in *Punch*, as a Christmas one for 1921, using the quote 'God rest you merry gentlemen, let nothing you dismay' –

> 'The turn of a tap and the striking of a match in each and every room will give that warmth and cheerfulness throughout the house, without which the mistress cannot 'rest merry' but will indeed be 'dismayed'.'

Inter-war advertising of gas and electric fires focused on quickness of response, range of heat dispersion, cleanliness, feeling of cosiness and cost to run. The criteria for choosing between electric fires were vague. Ferranti always inferred theirs had some unique quality but what this was, was never spelt out –

> 'I'm a Ferranti; others are made to look like me, but there the similarity ends.'

Cannon Gas Fires advertisement, *Punch*, 1935

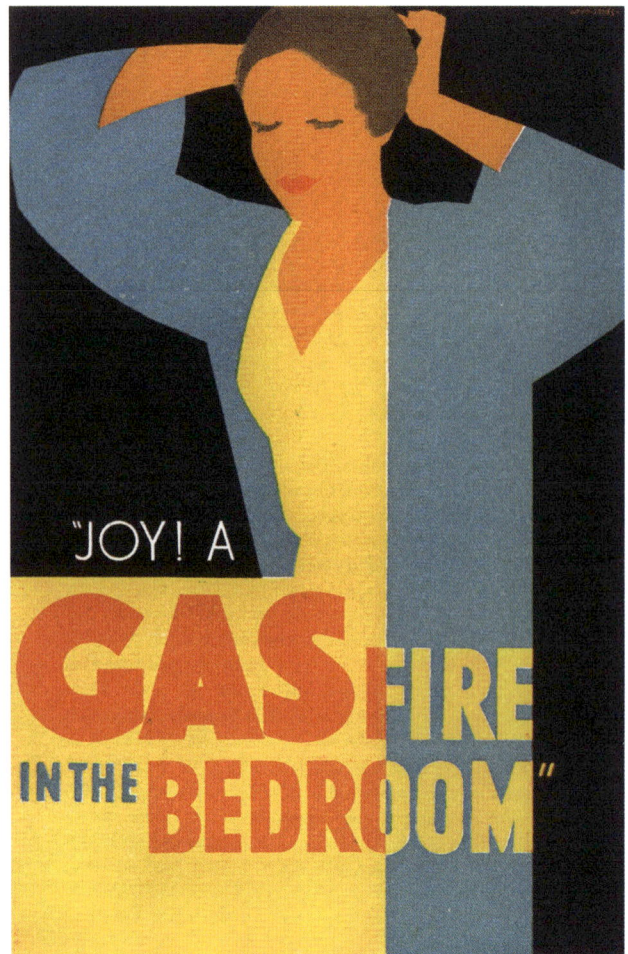

Commercial Art Magazine, 1936

Aesthetic design does not seem to have been a major advertising gambit albeit companies, from time to time, would use the word 'modern'. But, for a while, electric fires would come on to the market disguised as yachts, sunflowers, Egyptian pyramids and other such fancies. Nevertheless when a company decided to commission a designer and name him, this attracted a certain amount of publicity, as HMV with its Christian Barman electric heater, Wells Coates' variations on 'Thermovent' for EKCO, and the Gas Light and Coke Company's use of Misha Black for its 'Vek'.

Yet until the post-war years coal fires still dominated the living room, with gas or electric fires for the bedrooms, the latter having the versatile advantage of being easily portable as well as fixed. Even into the 1960s, such a mix was still being used to heat rooms as *Ideal Home* put it –

'Most houses are heated haphazardly. A coal fire here, paraffin heater there, electric radiator somewhere else.'

Ideal Home estimated that less than 10% of homes had central heating in Britain in 1962. Although a Russian is credited with developing the radiator in the mid-19th century, central heating was slow to catch on in Britain partly due to its expense but no doubt also due to the reluctance to give up some form of hearth. Heavy cast iron radiators eventually morphed into the slim ones of today and solid fuel, as a means of heating gave way to central heating systems run by liquid fuels, gas or electricity. Eventually the fireplace began to disappear, to be replaced by the

Gas Light and Coke Company advertisement, *Modern Publicity*, 1938

East Midlands Gas Board advertisement, *Modern Publicity*, 1955

 **Countess**

A new Countess fire in your home brings a feeling of warmth and luxury, its clean, neat lines and colourful elegance will change the appearance of the whole room. Choose from six attractive colour schemes.

No. 233 2 kW £6.19.1
No. 234 3 kW £7.19.9

18¼"w. × 19¾"h. × 7½"d. 13½ lb.

Guardsman Red (Black back).
Black (Guardsman Red back).
Bronze (Bronze back).

Finishes: Citron Yellow (Black back).
Sky Blue (Ivory back).
Cloud Grey (Guardsman Red back).

 Homeguard

The Homeguard has been designed for those who prefer a fire with specially protected elements. It incorporates a switch which automatically cuts off the current in the event of the fire being knocked over or lifted up, thus affording extra protection for both young and old. The fire is mounted on swivel feet so that it may be tilted to project heat at any angle.

No. 155 2 kW £13.3.4

19"w. × 19"h. × 9½"d. 19 lb.
Finishes: Silver Bronze, Ivory/Black.

 Melrose

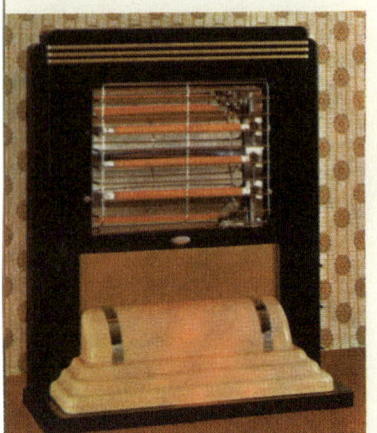

Large enough to cover any fireplace opening, the Melrose incorporates a beautifully designed translucent base to provide restful background lighting for your television viewing.

No. 274 3 kW £19.19.5

22⅛"w. × 26"h. × 8½"d. 24 lb.

Finishes: Two-tone Beige, Black/Gold.

Adam

The Adam style has been faithfully interpreted in this handsome fire. It is entirely handmade in cast aluminium, specially finished to give an antique appearance.

No. 915 2 kW £14.12.11

24"w. × 20½"h. × 7"d. 16 lb.

No. 916 3 kW £17.3.2

25½"w. × 22½"h. × 7½"d. 19 lb.

Finishes: Armour Bright (Rustless).

Belling leaflet, c1960

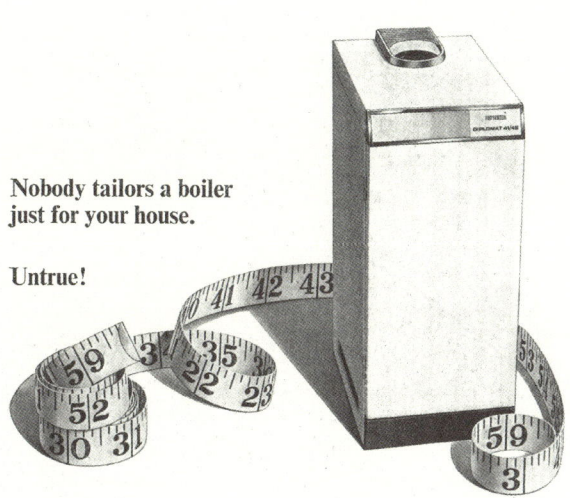

Potterton Boilers advertisement, *House Beautiful*, 1966

Crane Boilers advertisement, *Ideal Home*, 1966

Ascot advertisement, *Art and Industry*, 1938

Ascot advertisement, *Modern Publicity*, 1939

television set as the focus for the family [at least until mobiles and iPads began to separate them].

There was relatively little advertising of central heating systems in the general press or in women's and housekeeping magazines for the period covered by this book – the 1920s to the 1960s – although presumably more in the technical press aimed at builders and architects. Potterton's was the name most frequently to be seen. A typical Potterton advertisement would often take a full page with the top half a drawing or photograph, the bottom the copy. A striking one in *House Beautiful* in 1963 had an image of Rodin's 'The Thinker' on top of a Potterton boiler with the tag – 'A Potterton does your thinking for you'. The reader was offered five central heating programmes at the flip of a switch firing heating and hot water 'as you want it, at the times you want it'.

Of course when it came to hot water alone the most frequent advertiser in the inter-war years was Ascot. Dr. Bernard Freidman had actually been selling German water heaters for some years when, in 1933, he decided to change the name of his company to Ascot Gas Water Heaters. In the post-war years Ascot was eventually taken over by the Radiation Group but continued to use the trade name Ascot in advertisements. A scan of these, over the years, shows how it developed from a rather crude machine, through to its stream-lining, until it disappeared into a kitchen unit in the 60s.

Witney Earlywarm electric blankets advertisement, *Ideal Home*, 1962

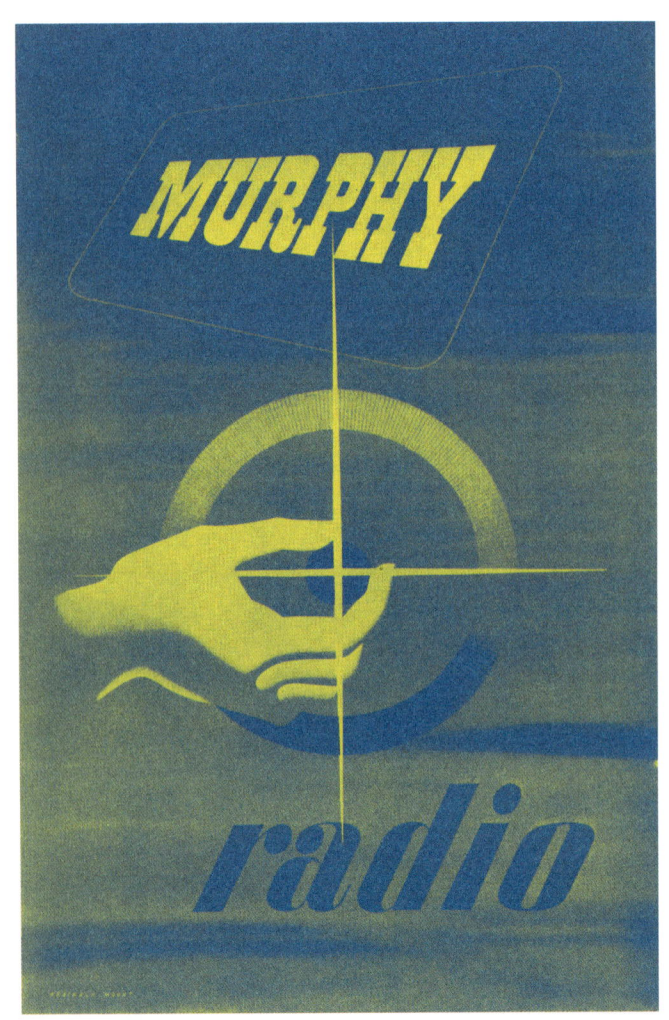
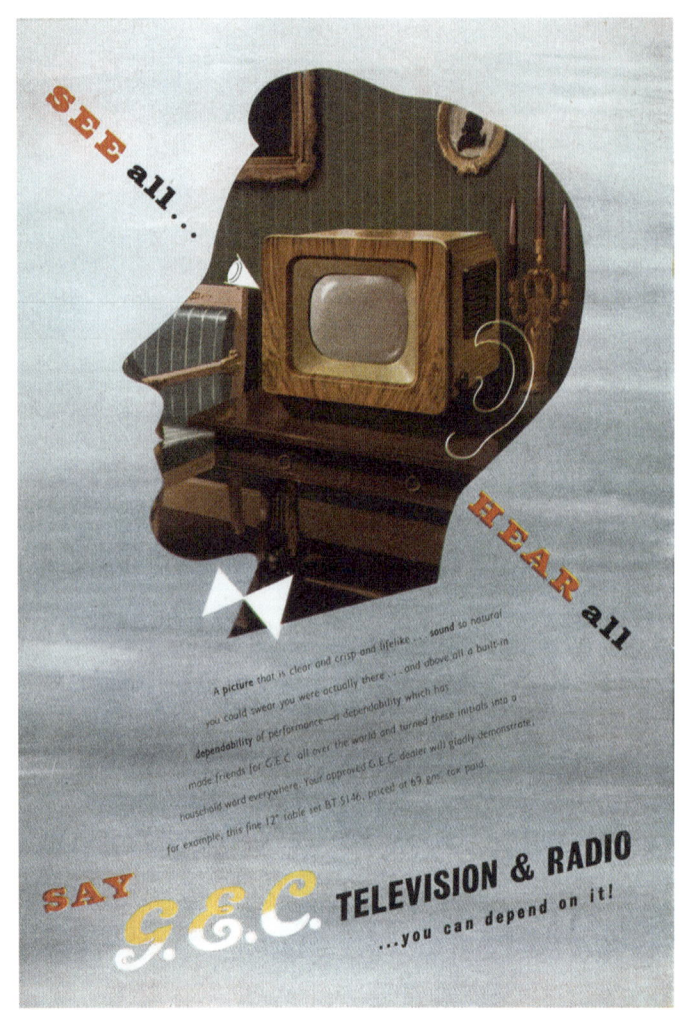

ENTERTAINMENT

The early 1920s saw the establishment of the BBC and the growth of the radio manufacturing industry, the two in parallel and closely interdependent – the manufacturers monitoring closely what was happening in broadcasting and how to modify their products accordingly, broadcasting dependent on the technical advances in the transmitting and reception of sound. The early basic crystal sets gave way to the cumbersome valve receivers, which, in turn, morphed into the compact all-in-one receivers of the early 30s. By then most of the major manufacturers in the field were operating – Ferranti, Pye, Western Electric, EKCO, Murphy, Mullard, HMV, Marconiphone, Decca, Thorn, Bush etc., some extending their range of products from allied fields as Mullard and Thorn from lamps, Decca from gramophones, and Pye from scientific instruments. Others, as EKCO, were born directly from the excitement and stimulation of the new technology of sending and receiving sound.

Certainly the early advertisements relating to the radio tended to be more about the selling of component parts to be attached to each other in the home than to anything resembling the wireless set on the market in the 30s. Radio was portrayed as a highly technical affair, largely to be handled by the man of the house. Typical was a Ferranti advertisement in 1928 advertising audio-frequency transformers, output transformers, voltmeters, loudspeakers, and so on. Marconiphone was similarly advertising its 'valves, receiving sets, loudspeakers, transformers, power units and other components'. In the early sets the speaker was separate from the receiver and much of the advertising was competitive as to who could produce the sleekest and slimmest improvements of the large horns, which tended to be cumbersome and take up much room. Typical was a claim made for the Sterling *Primax*, described as the hornless loudspeaker –

Western Electric poster stamp, 1923

Reginald Mount, Murphy Radio, 1946 & G.E.C. advertisement, *Art and Industry*, 1953

Western Electric Wireless advertisement, 1922

Fougasse. Columbia gramophone advertisement, *Punch*, 1927

'A charming aluminium standard together with a specially prepared diaphragm in place of the ordinary horn – the 'Primax' is therefore more artistic in reproduction and appearance.'

Curiously, many of these late 1920s advertisements showing people listening intently to what was coming out of the speaker, often grandly mounted on its own stand, had the listeners in evening dress as if 'listening in' was some special occasion, or possibly only available, at that time, to the class of person who 'dressed for dinner'.

By the late 20s and early 30s the speaker had become attached to the receiver, all encased in wood. To let the sound emerge, these wooden cases were much given to being fretworked – bars, grills and the like, so much so that they were characterised in the trade by such nicknames as 'Dartmoor' and 'Pentonville'! With the arrival of bakelite, the shape of the case was made from a mould, giving the designer greater freedom. EKCO were leaders in this employing Serge Chermayeff and Wells Coates, the young 'flavour of the month' designers of the time. EKCO's first radio casing designed by Wells Coates was shown at Radiolympia in 1934, advertised as 'white Bakelite with chromium fittings containing 8-stage superhet receiver with loudspeaker'. Wells Coates' sensational spherical radio became a best seller.

Murphy also turned to professional designers for its radios – to the brothers Gordon and Dick Russell. Both Murphy and Gordon Russell Ltd. were struggling financially at the beginning of the 1930s but by combining Murphy's technical prowess

His Master's Voice advertisement, *Punch*, 1935

with Dick Russell's designing originality the fortunes of both enterprises were revived. Murphy became one of the prominent players in advertising radio sets, using the advertising agency C.R.Casson.

From the beginning of radio manufacturing a major technical challenge was the adjusting of the receiver to get the particular station one needed – an activity commonly referred to as 'tuning in'. The family would sit in anxious expectation as the head of the household went about twiddling the relevant knobs until a crackling became a recognisable sound, a human voice or music. There was much made, in advertisements, of anything that could ease the process of 'tuning in' as in an advertisement for a Lissin set, in 1933 –

His Master's Voice 'show train', *Art and Industry*, c1930s

'One knob tuning control – as you turn it the stations come in automatically.'

EKCO was one of the first to introduce a dial marked with the names of the stations and even as late as 1942 one of its advertisements was still making much of its spearhead work when it came to tuning –

'EKCO were the first in this country with Motorised Press-buton Tuning, the amazing simplification of accurate radio control.'

Some radio manufacturers had their own or specified retail outlets – their dealers – and they would supply displays for windows and interiors of the shops to show off their latest models. HMV had a major retail outlet in Oxford Street, which advertised its design consciousness by having its building designed by the famous architect Joseph Emberton. It also supplied its dealers with stands and sent out monthly posters to be slotted into them. It had its own advertising and display workshops providing a constant flow of publicity material. Other manufacturers would also supply displays to their dealers and might add ideas for the dealers to work on themselves as Murphy did in its dealers' news-sheet *Murphy News*, and Marconi did in its publication *Window Ideas*.

The 30s also saw several radio manufacturers making a start in the use of 'names' in their advertising to endorse their products. Particularly frequent was Bush's use of Christopher

Stone, who has been described as the first radio disc jockey. Bush thought to use him as someone with a common touch [despite his Eton education], talking directly to the reader, as in one of their immediate post-war advertisements –

> *'I was told by the Bush engineers that their new Bi-focal circuit levels out the response curve of the receiver. Well, that may mean something to you but it means precious little to me – until I heard the circuit in action.'*

EKCO also used 'names' from the 1930s onwards; in one of its pre-war advertisements it showed the glamorous faces of 'wives of famous broadcasters who chose EKCO' – Fred Hartley [conductor of light music], Arthur Askey [comedian], Tommy Trinder [comedian] and George Formby [comedian].

Of course all manufacturers' advertising changed with the onset of war. The message then communicated was that firms were changing to the manufacture of essential goods, that the listener would get news of what was going on all over the world via their radio sets, that those who had purchased well would not have maintenance problems during the war, and that great new models would be coming onto the market 'when peace broke out'. Some typical examples were – for Murphy –

> *'Millions of people will remember gratefully the wireless sets that brought them the steadying and*

EKCO advertisement, *Picture Post*, 1939

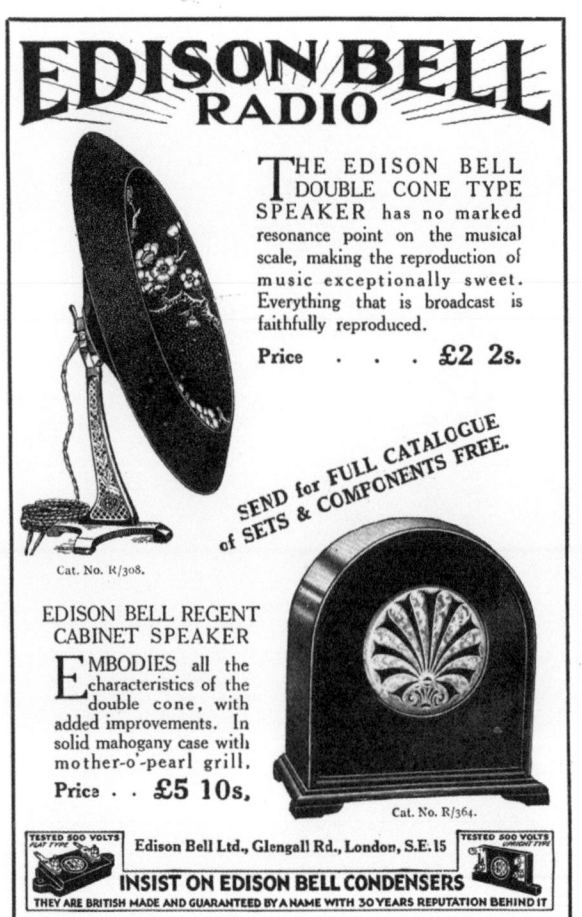

Edison Bell advertisement, *BBC Handbook*, 1928

Mullard advertisement, *Picture Post*, 1942

ENTERTAINMENT

Radio Rentals advertisement, *Picture Post*, 1945

Roberts' Radio advertisement, *BBC Yearbook*, 1952

inspiring voice of our Prime Minister. Brought them courage and humour…Brought them guidance and diversion when they were most needed.'

for Philips –

'Only of one thing can we be certain: that whatever happens and in whichever corner of the world it takes place, you will hear it immediately on all-wave radio. From Rome, Paris or Moscow comes the news. From America comes informed, uncensored comment on the news. And with a 1940 Philips, you get it all. today you can listen to history being made.'

for EKCO –

'When 'domestic radio' is once more our main concern EKCO will still be there – leading the Industry.'

Although in the immediate post-war years there was a certain amount of advertising of radios, the manufacturers had begun to shift their focus to television. For this several firms resorted to the use of humour, a rarity in selling in the industry, as an EKCO advertisement in *Lilliput* in 1946 involving Oliver Cromwell! –

'Remove that bauble!' Cromwell said
'I think it's out of place.'
The hist'ry books all tell us that
He pointed to the mace.
The truth? The Common's radio
The worst he'd ever met –
'Take it away!' yelled Oliver
'And get an EKCO set!'

Ferranti used less whimsy in a 1947 advertisement with an image of a dour Dr. Johnson and a young trumpet player –

'You can hear whichever you like with equal realism on a Ferranti receiver. The roll and rumble of Dr. Johnson's prose – or the tearing ecstasy of a trumpet-break…'

In addition to competitive advertising, individual manufacturers did combine forces, once a year, to exhibit their latest wares at Olympia. Radiolympia [which became popularly known as the Radio Show] was first mounted in 1926 and from that a body was established to represent all British manufacturers – the Radio Manufacturers' Association – which ran the show annually until the war. It was reconstituted in 1944 as the British Radio Equipment Manufacturers' Association [BREMA] with some 150 members showing annually. One report gave a somewhat jaundiced view of the yearly scene –

'The noise enveloped one; it was wearying and tiresome. The Main Hall was a confused blaze of neon and strip lighting. There was so much light everywhere that any individual scheme was deprived of effect, swallowed up in the general blaze.'

ENTERTAINMENT

Radiolympia first showed off television in the late 20s. In fact broadcasting by radio had barely become established before manufacturers began to experiment with the possibilities of television, the Baird mechanical television set appearing at Olympia in 1929. The BBC put out its first television broadcast in 1936 and the likes of Mullard, Pye, Decca and EKCO were all experimenting with cathode ray based models by then. It is estimated that between 1937 and 1939 some 3000 television sets were sold in Britain, and Thorn was beginning to rent out televisions as well as radios. By the late 40s Pye was to dominate the television market to eventually be overtaken by Thorn in the 1960s.

Early television sets were quite sensitive to atmosphere – a change in the voltage in the electricity supply or a plane flying overhead. In fact, paradoxically EKCO's attempts to advertise Ekcovision by attaching a banner behind a plane had to be halted for the very reason that it interfered with reception in households beneath the flight path!

When it came to advertising televisions, 'size' seems to have been all important. Initially the concern was the size of the screen, for many of the early sets although in large fretworked show-off cabinets, had very small screens. Manufacturers frog-leapt each other in their advertisements as to the dimensions of their latest offering. Typical were the Hale Television advertisements in the 50s, pointing out that its screens were now of the size that a whole family could watch at ease together. Philips hired in 'our Grace' – Gracie Fields – and had her exclaiming in her Lancashire way – 'Philip's big picture television is champion'. To current owners of

Radio Manufacturers' Association advertisement, *Modern Publicity*, 1939–40

Murphy Television advertisements designed by F.H.K. Henrion, 1948

Pye advertisement, *Lilliput*, 1949

John Bainbridge, Pye advertisement, *Art and Industry*, 1952

a television set that dominates a wall, it must seem curious to read of Gracie's enthusiasm – 'you, your family and more of your friends can enjoy the programmes in much greater comfort.'

By the 1960s when television screens had been freed from their cumbersome cabinets, 'size' became a matter not so much of screen dimension [albeit this continued to be a competitive criterion], but of screen 'slimness' – Pye claimed 'inches slimmer', EKCO 'slimmest ever', whilst Philips actually named its set 'Slenderamic'.

In terms of excellence of design of radio and television press advertising Murphy stood out clearly from the others, certainly in the post-war years. It was one of the few manufacturers in the industry to have the design standard of its advertisements recognised in the design press when, via its advertising agency C.R.Casson Ltd., *Designers in Britain* featured a remarkable example for Murphy Radio designed by Reginald Mount, who had produced much distinguished work for the Ministry of Information during the war. *Modern Publicity* for 1952-3 showed another outstanding Murphy image, this time by Abram Games, the leading graphic designer of the time; and at much the same period Murphy was also commissioning F.H.K.Henrion, a designer of much the same status. All these advertisements stood out from the general outpouring from the industry by their total absence, or very sparse appearance, of copy, or of hype, merely having a dominating image of a set accompanied by striking typography for 'Murphy Radio' or 'Murphy Television', as appropriate.

Philips advertisement, *BBC Handbook*, 1960

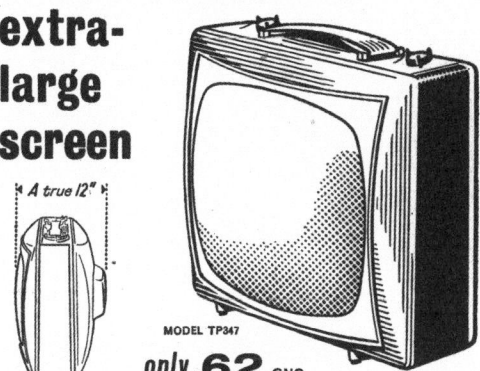

EKCO advertisement, *BBC Handbook*, 1960

His Master's Voice advertisement, *Punch*, 1939

The gramophone, as a form of home entertainment, of course had been more popular earlier than the radio, but had been worked by the power of the human hand winding a handle. By WWI Emile Berliner had set up a London branch of his company and had purchased the trademark His Master's Voice [whose dog, listening loyally to what was coming out of a horn, appeared on all its advertising]; and shellac had been found to be the most effective material for discs. By the late 30s wireless sets were on the market with integral gramophones, and the radiogram emerged, large, heavy and adding grandeur to the living room. A 1939 advertisement for an HMV autoradiogram gives some idea of the pomposity of the design that many early 'music centre' cabinets could achieve and the status they strutted in their bulk. This particular model offered 'unsurpassed tonal realism', but also the novelty of the gramophone changing its own records. Forward some 20 years and the music centre was being sold with its constituent parts either in one case, such as the B&O Beomaster and the Braun, or as separate units as Philips Audio Plan, all of which shouted 'good taste' in the puritan simplicity of their design. B&O in its 1960s advertising of its Beomaster [referred to as a stereogram], made much of the design features declaring it was meant for 'discriminating people', for 'those who value design and quality above price' – as with so many powered domestic appliances, the look of the thing had come to be as important as the way it functioned.

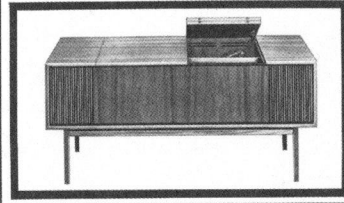
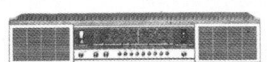

Bang and Olufsen advertisement, *Ideal Home*, 1966

Philips advertisement, *Ideal Home*, 1968

EPILOGUE

From any collection of advertising ephemera, if chronologically sorted, one can learn something of graphic design history as typographic style, use of colour, the proportion of copy to image, the use of photomontage, and so on; but in addition one can appreciate the development of the product being advertised and also aspects of the society consuming the product.

When it comes to powered domestic products, a quick overview of advertisements shows that many early examples were merely power being attached externally to what was already being used for cooking, cleaning etc. as gas piped to a stove or an electric motor on the outside of a wash tub. Over time the power became integral to the appliance, hidden within it. And eventually, although the technical functioning was ever key, the design of a product and its contribution to a 'lifestyle' became increasingly important; domestic appliances became a part of 'interior design'.

Of what powered domestic appliance advertising tells about how society was changing over the period of the book – 1920 to 1970 – it is difficult to avoid the obvious – the relative roles of men and women in any household. The man, over the whole period, is portrayed as the breadwinner – it is he who earns the money and he who decides generously to bestow, to the always 'delighted' wife, the latest appliance, for her birthday or for Christmas. If he is to be seen at all in advertisements he almost certainly is sitting in an armchair with his feet up after a hard day's work, smoking his pipe and reading the newspaper. Occasionally he may also put in an appearance as the household's technical expert, for it was assumed he would know more about how machinery worked than his wife who was using it daily.

Cassandre 'electric power', Holland, 1930

Hot Water by Wire, information booklet, 1930s

It is true that, over the years, the women do change their occupational uniforms from wrap around aprons to frilly hostess ones, but if powered domestic appliances relieved them of drudgery, as so many of the advertisements boasted, it was not for them to have careers or to make contributions to society, but to shop and gossip. Indeed, some feminist writers would hold that the appliances enforced a greater drudgery – that of having to be a domestic goddess. Many of these writers are not of the age to have hand wrung out sheets in the yard or daily cleared ashes from the grate. The reduction of drudgery has been no small matter. Possibly they have found support for their argument because most women appearing in these advertisements seem to be middle class, and so the advertising reflects the roles such women chose, or were obliged to adopt. Of course they would need to be comfortably off to afford the expense of new products coming on to the market. They are seen occasionally in evening clothes, even joyfully opening the new refrigerator; and freed by the thermostat, they shop or coffee morning, usually shown in the most stylish clothes and rarely if ever in a work environment. There certainly was a good deal, in the advertising, of how possessing state of the art powered domestic products endowed status; the advertising of the products was not so much 'keeping up with the Joneses' as 'being' the Joneses, ahead of the field.

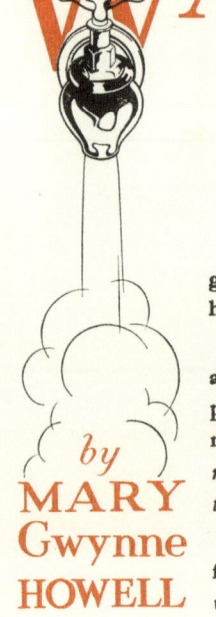

EPILOGUE

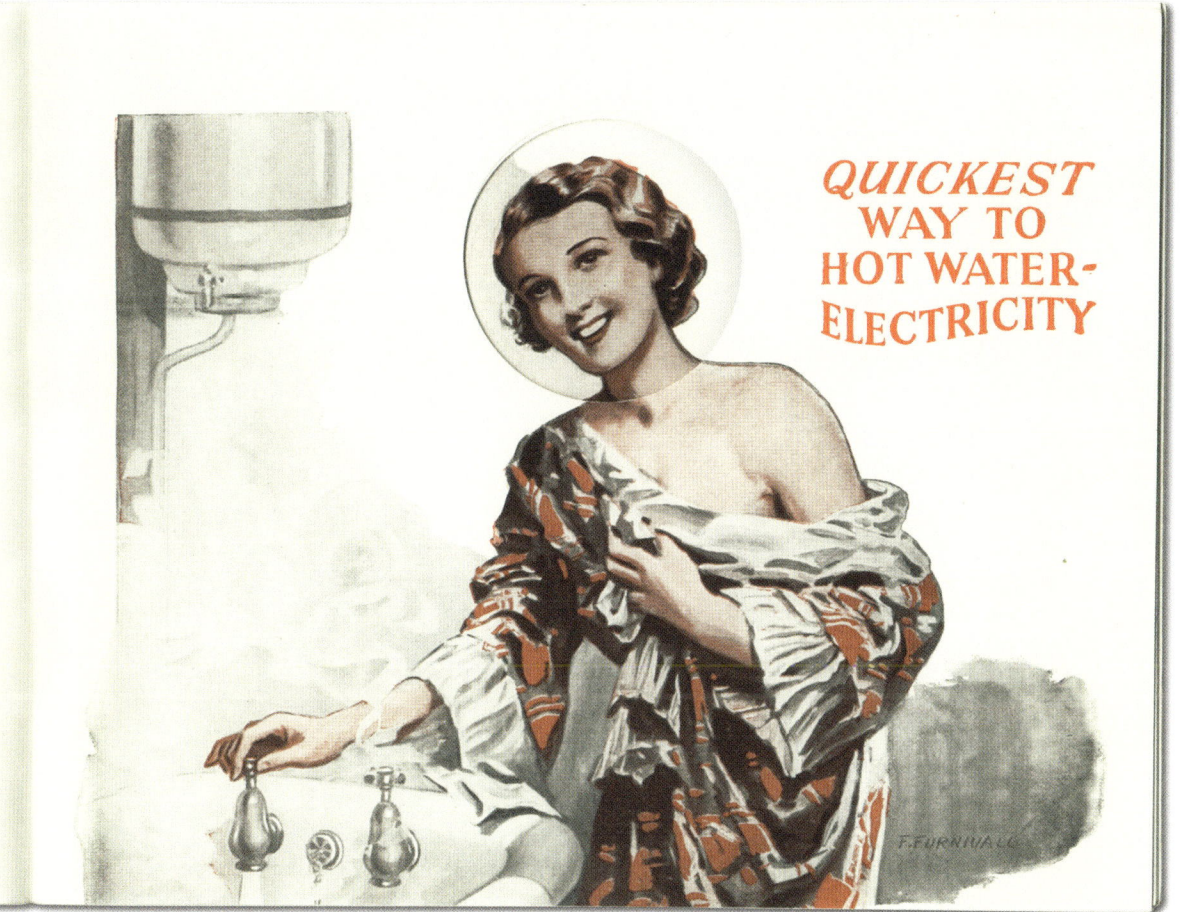

TER
wire

grumbling his way
breakfast, snapping
ne, and going off
in a thoroughly bad
And when things
hroughout the day
why!

such a state of
oidable in a well-
sehold. There is no
chances, for *electricity*
ater a certainty first
rning.

supply of hot water
family can be relied
lectric water heating

QUICKEST WAY TO HOT WATER— ELECTRICITY

BIBLIOGRAPHY

1934   Peggy Scott *An Electrical Adventure*
           Electrical Association for Women

1964   Lawrence Wright *Home Fires Burning, the history of domestic heating and cooking*
           Routledge & Kegan Paul

1980   Malcolm Peebles *Evolution of the Gas Industry*
           Macmillan

1981   Anthony Byers *Centenary of Service, a history of electricity in the home*
           The Electricity Council

1986   Caroline Davidson *A woman's work is never done*
           Chatto & Windus

1987   Penny Sparke *Electrical Appliances*
           Unwin Hyman

1998   Bob Gordon *Early Electrical Appliances*
           Shire Publications

1999   Anthony Rowley *The Book of Kitchens*
           Flammarion

2004   Anne Glendenning *Demons of Domesticity*
           Ashgate

2007   David J. Eveleigh *A History of the Kitchen*
           Sutton Publishing

2007   Robin Wyatt *Glowing with Warmth*
           Journal 31, *Decorative Arts Society*

2012   Kathryn Ferry *The 1950s Kitchen*
           Shire Publications

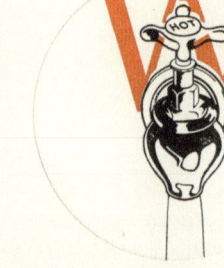

upon the hot
pply: first the
st be really hot,
dly it must not
pecial heating for
in hand.

ctric water heater
th of these con-
ust a turn of the
here is all the hot
want. I consider
factor in "dish-
hot water sterilises
leanses.

plates and dishes
nse in really hot
g touch, they are
the rack and will

"sudsy" water,
water, and dried
ave a sheen equal

QUICKEST WAY TO HOT WATER— ELECTRICITY